A NOTE FROM DEMI

"Follow your heart as long as you live. . . .
Bring your whole heart towards excellence. . . .
And no limit may be set to art."
—*The Instruction of Ptahhotop, 2200 BCE*

Inspired by the exquisite line in Egyptian paintings, pyramids, royal temples, sanctuaries of the gods, mastabas, sculpture, and jewelry, I painted King Tut. I used Egyptian and Chinese inks and Asian brushes. Inspired also by the Egyptians' dazzling gold and their never-ending quest for eternity, I created the borders and frames with Egyptian designs of gold and jewels.

Of the numerous books I read, *Tutankhamun: The Life and Death of the Boy King* by Christine El Mahdy, St. Martin's Press, 1999, was the most impressive because of its marvelous portrait of Tutankhamun and the historical significance of his life.

Other Tutankhamun treasures were all the books by Sir Ernest A. Wallis Budge: *Tutankhamun, The Gods of the Egyptians, Egyptian Magic, Egyptian Ideas of the Afterlife, Egyptian Language,* and *The Dwellers of the Nile.* Also *Tutankhamun* by Christiane Desroches-Noblecourt, New York Graphics Society, 1963; *Treasures of Tutankhamun,* Metropolitan Museum of Art, 1976; *The Complete Tutankhamun* by Nicholas Reeves, Thames and Hudson, 1995; *Tutankhamun* by Aude Gros de Beler, Moliere, Paris, 2001; and *Tutankhamun* by T. G. H. James, Friedman/Fairfax Publishers, Italy, 2000. When I read material in which scholars disagreed, such as on the date of King Tutankhamun's death, I used the information that most sources accepted.

Marshall Cavendish Corporation 99 White Plains Road Tarrytown, NY 10591 www.marshallcavendish.us/kids

The quote, "going with Aten before him," on page 9 is on the dream stela in front of the Sphinx.

Thanks to Dr. Elizabeth A. Waraksa, Ph.D., CLIR Postdoctoral Fellow,
11360B Charles E. Young Research Library, UCLA, for evaluating the text and artwork.

LIBRARY OF CONGRESS CATALOGING-IN-PUBLICATION DATA Demi Tutankhamun / Demi. p. cm. ISBN 978-0-7614-5558-5
1. Tutankhamen, King of Egypt—Juvenile literature. 2. Egypt—History—Nineteenth dynasty, ca. 1320-1200 B.C.—Juvenile literature.
3. Pharaohs—Biography—Juvenile literature. I. Title. DT87.5.D36 2008 932'.014092—dc22 [B] 2008029313

The illustrations are rendered in mixed media. Book design by Michael Nelson Editor: Margery Cuyler
Printed in Malaysia First edition
1 3 5 6 4 2

mc Marshall Cavendish Children

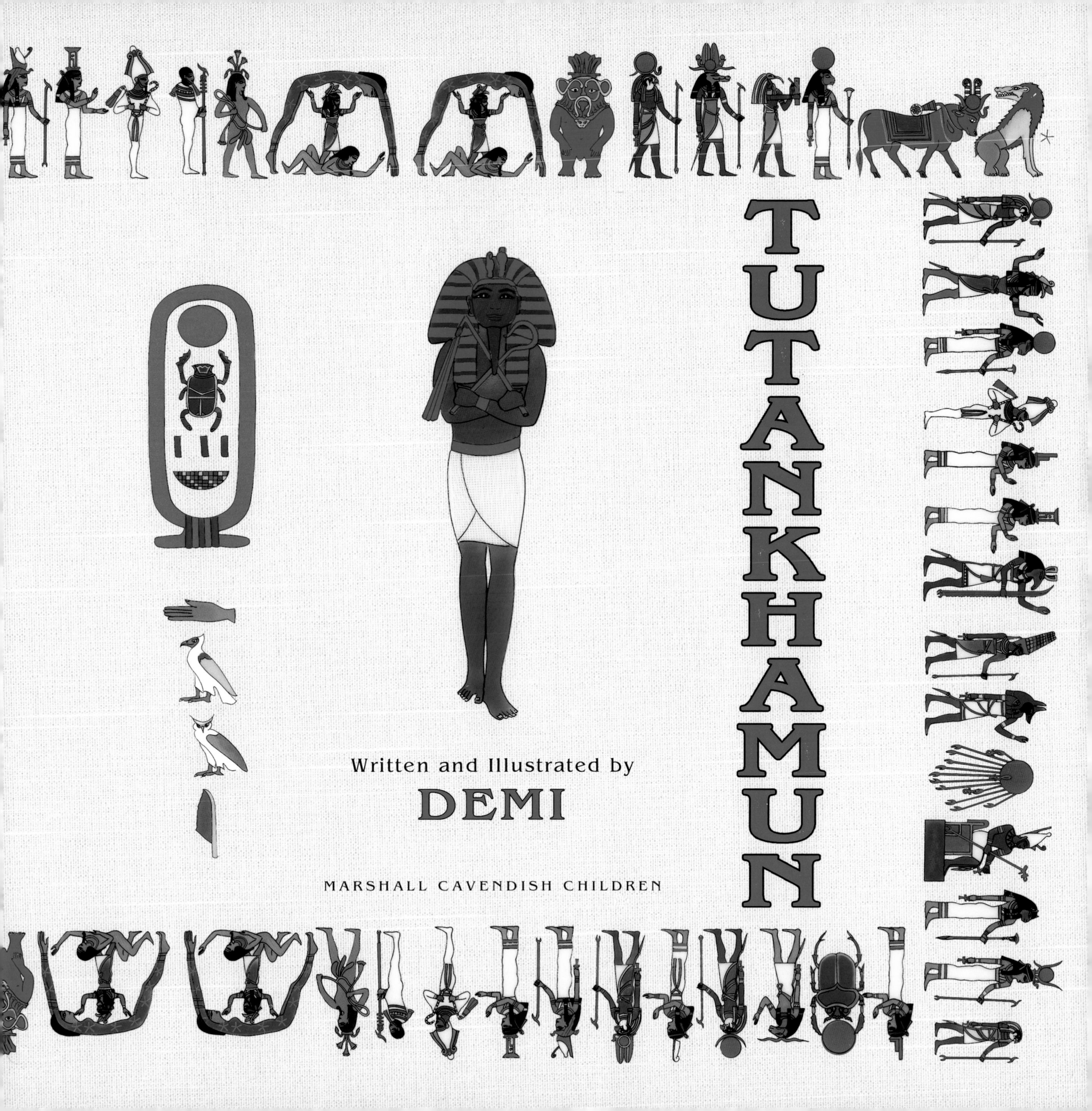

TUTANKHAMUN

Written and Illustrated by

DEMI

MARSHALL CAVENDISH CHILDREN

"O, Egypt—how beautiful indeed is the sight;
How pleasant indeed is the view!"

—Ancient Egyptian verse

KING THUTMOSE IV,

who ruled from 1419 to 1386 BCE, was the great-grandfather of King Tutankhamun. As a young prince, Thutmose IV had many brothers and half-brothers who wanted to seize the throne. One day, he went out hunting in the desert and fell asleep in the shadow of the Sphinx. All of a sudden, he had an amazing dream in which he could see the Sphinx heaving and struggling in vain to throw off the sand that was burying its body. The great Sphinx said to him: "I am the sun god and your father. Listen and hear how you shall be ruler of all of Egypt. If you will clear away the sand that is burying my body, you will become king. I will be with you always. I will be near you and make you great!"

When Thutmose IV awoke, he immediately ordered the sand removed. He knew the divine power of the sun god was inside him and that he would become king. In gratitude, he vowed to worship the sun, Aten, and from then on, everything he did in his life would be "going with Aten before him."

Most Egyptians worshiped a sun god named Amun. Sometimes they worshiped Amun as a human, sometimes as an animal, and sometimes as a human with an animal head.

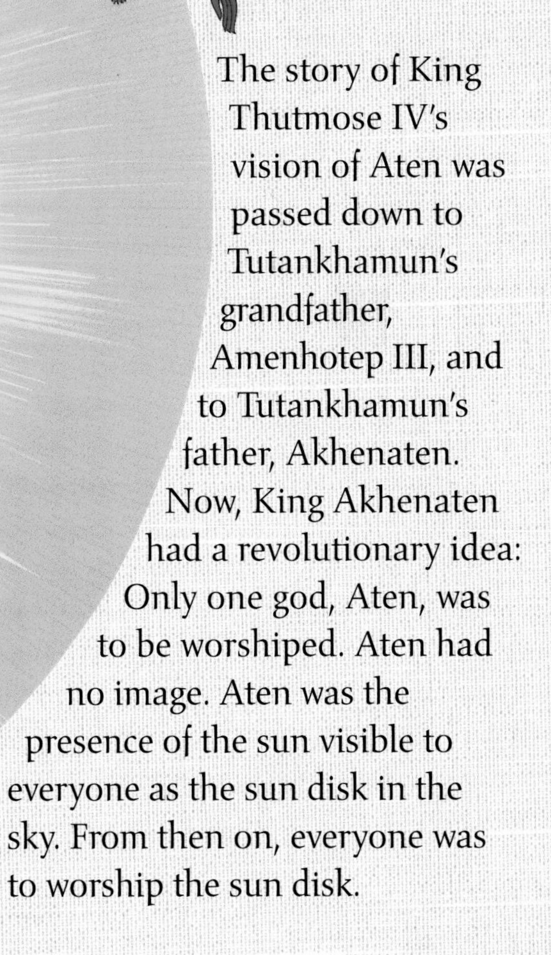

The story of King Thutmose IV's vision of Aten was passed down to Tutankhamun's grandfather, Amenhotep III, and to Tutankhamun's father, Akhenaten. Now, King Akhenaten had a revolutionary idea: Only one god, Aten, was to be worshiped. Aten had no image. Aten was the presence of the sun visible to everyone as the sun disk in the sky. From then on, everyone was to worship the sun disk.

Akenaten did not care about
Amun and the other gods.
He closed the temples of Amun.
This threatened and angered
the powerful Amun priests
and upset the people
who worshiped Amun.

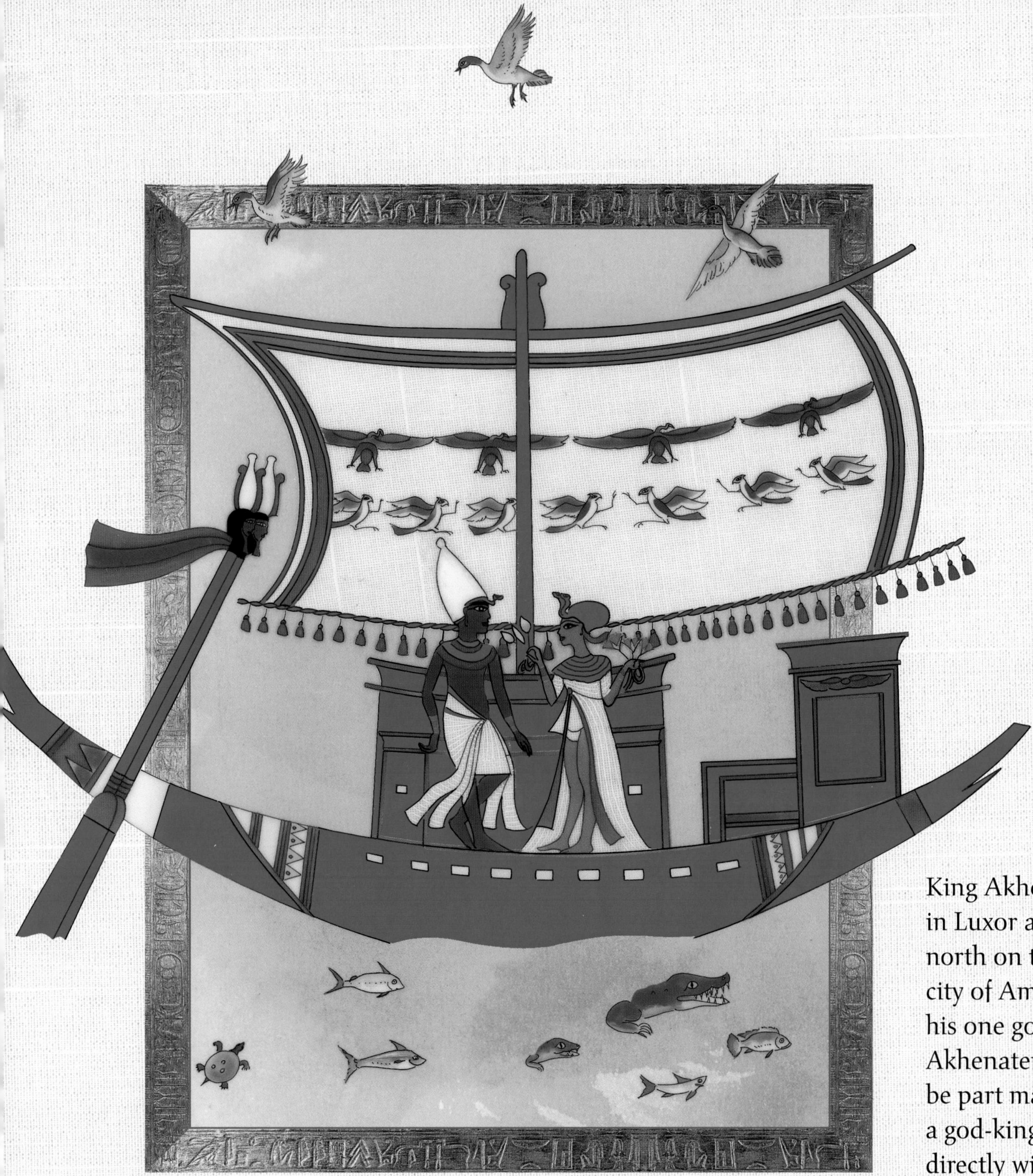

King Akhenaten left his palace in Luxor and sailed 200 miles north on the Nile to create the city of Amarna for himself and his one god, Aten. As a pharaoh, Akhenaten was considered to be part man and part god—a god-king who could communicate directly with Aten.

In the year 1342 BCE, in the city of Amarna, on the banks of the Nile, the future king Tutankhamun was born.

His father was the king and pharaoh Akhenaten, and his mother was believed to be a minor queen named Kiya. At birth, the child was given the name Tutankhaten.

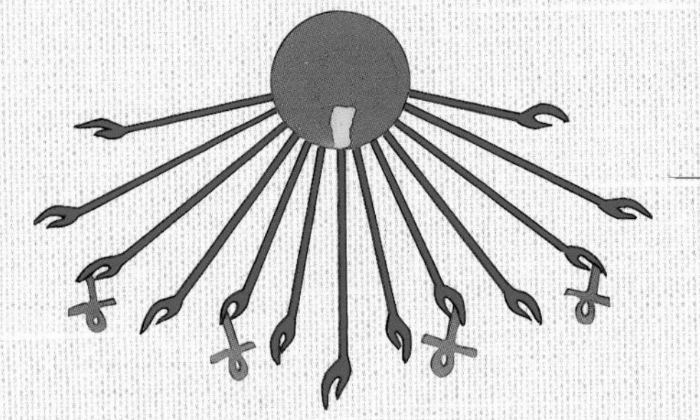

Prince Tutankhaten began his life praying to the sun disk, Aten. The Great Hymn to Aten says:

Splendid you rise in heaven's
lightland. . .
You fill every land with your
beauty . . .
when you shine as Aten of daytime;
as you dispel the dark,
as you cast your rays
[all Egypt is] in festivity.
Awake, they stand on their feet . . .
their arms adore your appearance . . .
all beasts browse on their herbs;
trees, herbs are sprouting,

birds fly from their nests,
their wings greeting your spirit.
All flocks frisk on their feet,
all that fly up and alight.
They live when you dawn for them. . . .
The fish in the river dart before you,
your rays are in the midst of
the sea. . . .
How many are your deeds,
though hidden from sight.
O Sole God beside whom there
is none! . . .
How excellent are your ways,
O Lord of Eternity! . . .
You are in my heart.

As a little prince, Tutankhaten watched the building of the great holy city of Amarna and the many temples for worshiping Aten. These were wide open spaces to the sun, not like the covered, dark, and hidden temples to Amun.

Prince Tutankhaten had many half-sisters and half-brothers, but most important were his six half-sisters. They were the children of his father and his beautiful major queen, Nefertiti. Tutankhaten especially loved his father's mother, Queen Tiye, who greatly protected and cared for him.

Prince Tutankhaten learned to read and write late Egyptian and to master algebra. He studied astronomy and the science of the stars. He read the Pyramid Texts, the Coffin Texts, and the Wisdom Literature of the great Egyptians.

This wisdom was based on understanding the needs of other people. It taught: Today you may be rich, but tomorrow you may be poor, so it is your duty to be kind and caring. Everyone is accountable to those above, like the king, and to those below, like the poor.

When Prince Tutankhaten was four, he joined the royal ostrich hunts and lion hunts and brought along his pet dog.

When he was older, he hunted for deer and wild ibex.

He practiced warfare with his bows, arrows, and lances.

For quiet fun, the prince played the Egyptian board game of senet, listened to the music of the harp, lute, and trumpet, and watched acrobats and colorful dancers.

When Prince Tutankhaten was about nine, his father, King Akhenaten, died. Suddenly Prince Tutankhaten was returned to the city of Luxor and crowned king and pharaoh in the temple of Karnak.

Two old men, Ay and Horemheb, held the real power to the throne. The young king Tutankhaten was a puppet in their hands.

Ay was the father of Queen Nefertiti and worshiped Aten. He truly loved and protected the young king and took the title Regent of Upper Egypt.

Horemheb was the commander of the army and the enemy of the young king. He worshiped Amun and took the title Regent of Lower Egypt. Horemheb made the young king change his name from Tutankhaten to Tutankhamun and worship Amun, the god his father had rebelled against.

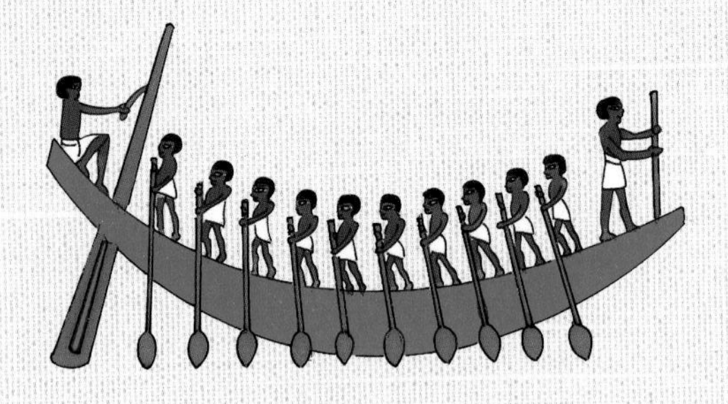

As a regent for the young king, Horemheb had to protect him. He took King Tutankhamun down the Nile to Memphis where he made the king restore the statues of the old gods and worship Amun.

Soon Ay insisted the king live under his protection part of the time, so King Tutankhamun was returned to Amarna.

There he married Ankhesenpaaten and named her his great royal wife. She was his half-sister and one of the daughters of Akhenaten and Queen Nefertiti.

The young king and queen then sailed south to Luxor. Amarna, the city of King Tutankhamun's father, was abandoned forever. In the temples of Luxor and Karnak, the king restored the worship of Amun, but he allowed the people to worship Aten, too.

He restored the Opet Festival, which celebrated all the gods with food and drink, and which the people loved. Now there was freedom of worship, and King Tutankhamun had made peace with both sides.

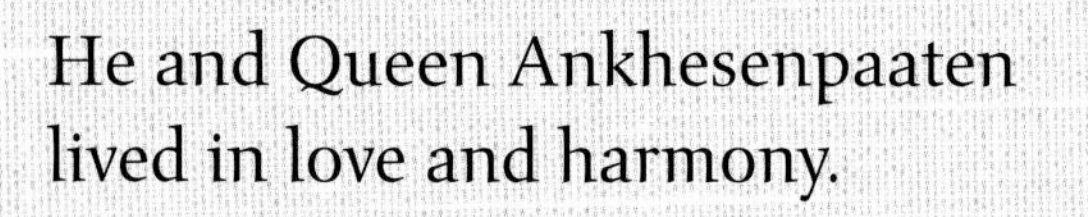

He and Queen Ankhesenpaaten
lived in love and harmony.

As was the practice of kings, Tutankhamun began building his burial temple on the west bank of the Nile near that of his grandfather, Amenhotep III, and his mother, Kiya.

At twelve, King Tutankhamun gave orders to the overseer of the tombs in the Valley of the Kings for the reburial of his beloved grandmother, Queen Tiye.

This overseer of tombs was a remarkable man named Maya. Later he was to prove his complete loyalty to Tutankhamun at the time of the king's death.

The Hittite warriors in the north were threatening Tutankhamun's kingdom. Horemheb, the commander of the Egyptian army, was constantly fighting them.

The king left behind no children, so there was no one to inherit the throne. Ay and Horemheb, the rulers of Upper and Lower Egypt, would each want to take control of the kingdom once they heard of Tutankhamun's death.

Ay heard about the king's death first. He did not tell Horemheb that King Tutankhamun had died.

Instead he schemed a devious plot to keep Horemheb away. He had Tutankhamun's widow, Ankhesenpaaten, write desperate letters to the Hittite king. She begged the king to send his son immediately to Egypt to marry her so her next marriage would not have to be to a commoner.

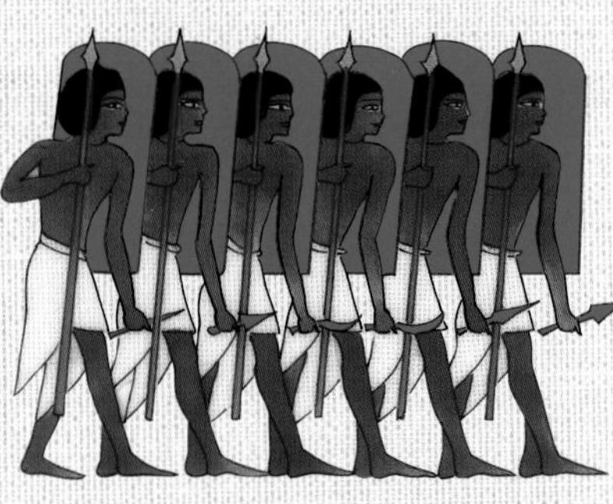

Horemheb discovered some of the messages going back and forth between the Hittites and the Egyptian queen. He killed the Hittite prince and his entire army before they could even meet the queen.

King Tutankhamun began collecting taxes to mount a great campaign against the Hittite army. But that campaign never happened.

At age nineteen, King
Tutankhamun suddenly died.
Some say he was murdered
by a blow behind his left ear;
some say he died in a hunting
accident; some say from a
tumor or an infection.
No one knows for sure.

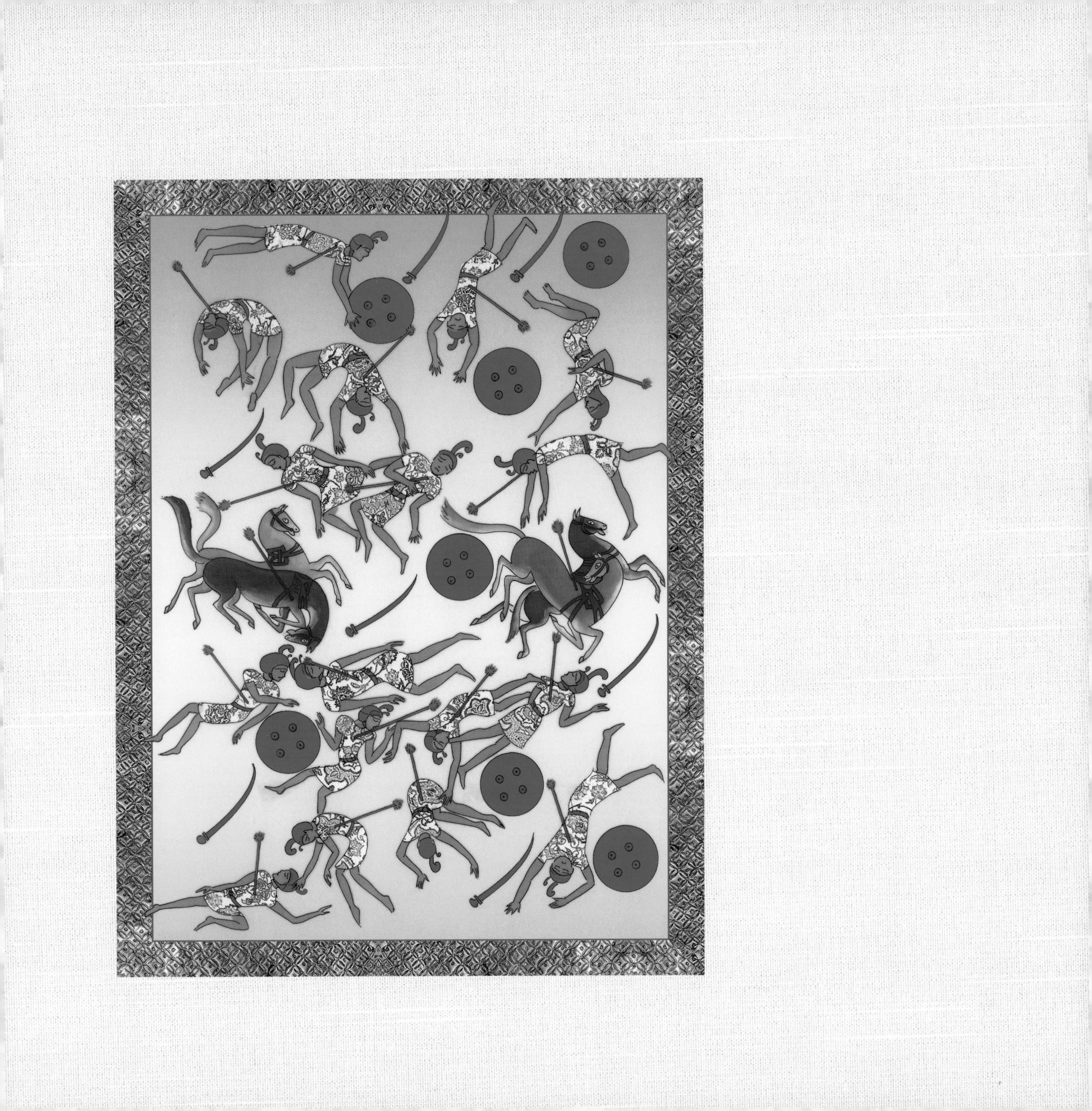

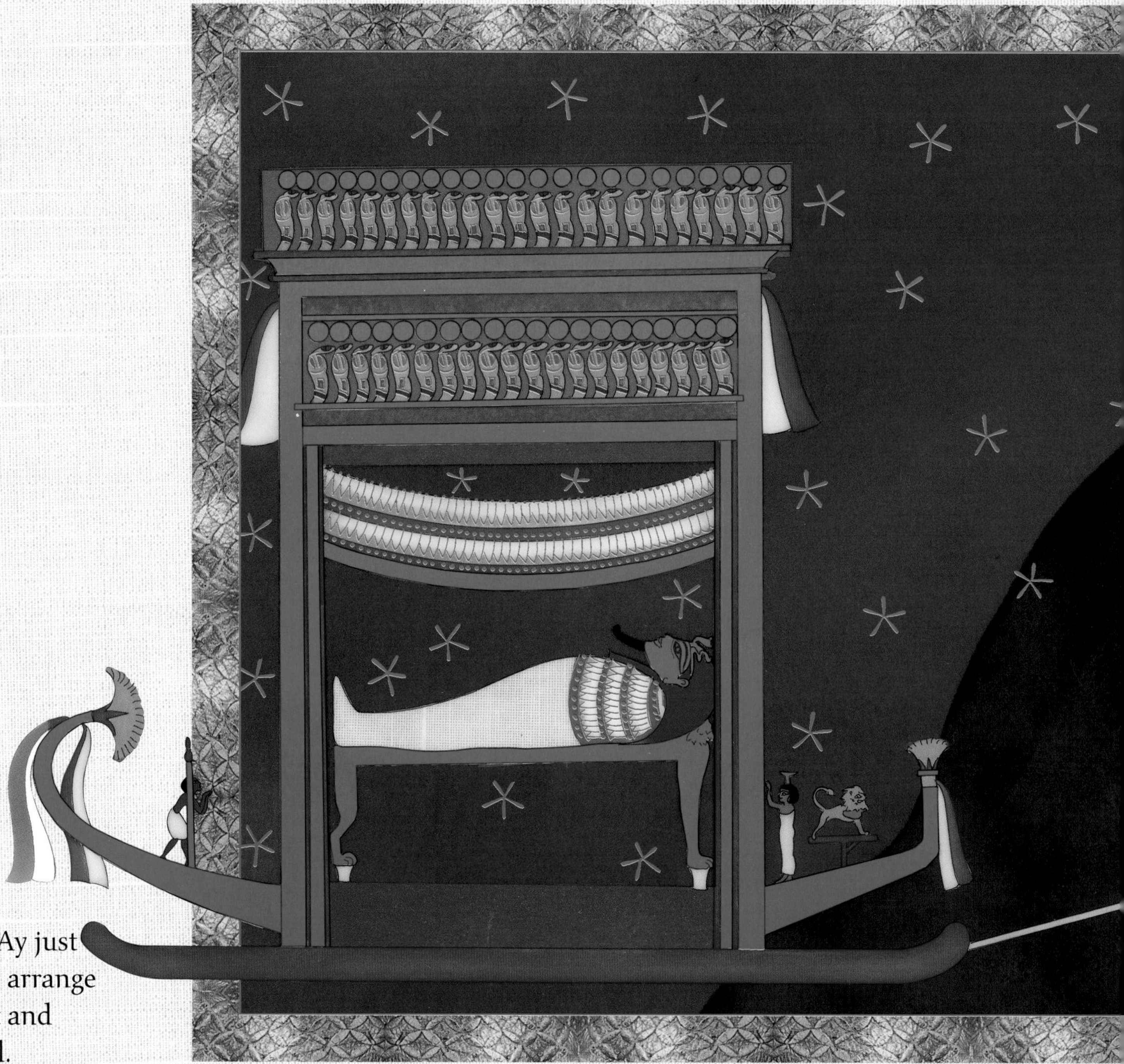

All this intrigue gave Ay just the time he needed to arrange Tutankhamun's secret and extremely hasty burial.

Maya, the most loyal overseer of tombs, swore he would never tell anyone the secret resting site of Tutankhamun, and he never did. For 3,249 years the secret survived.

In the tomb, Ay performed the Opening of the Mouth Ceremony, restoring and transforming the king into a perfect being. Now the king would travel to the afterworld and live in eternity.

By performing the Opening of the Mouth Ceremony, which could only be conducted by the person who would become the next king, Ay made himself heir to King Tutankhamun.

When Ay died, Horemheb instantly grabbed the throne. All the Amarna family were now dead, and Horemheb made sure they would be forgotten forever. He destroyed the great city of Amarna until not one stone stood upon another.

He struck the Amarna names of Akhenaten, Nefertiti, and Ay from every pillar. He destroyed the body and tomb of Ay, and he deliberately destroyed everything connected with the worship of Aten. But he could not destroy one thing: the lost tomb of Tutankhamun.

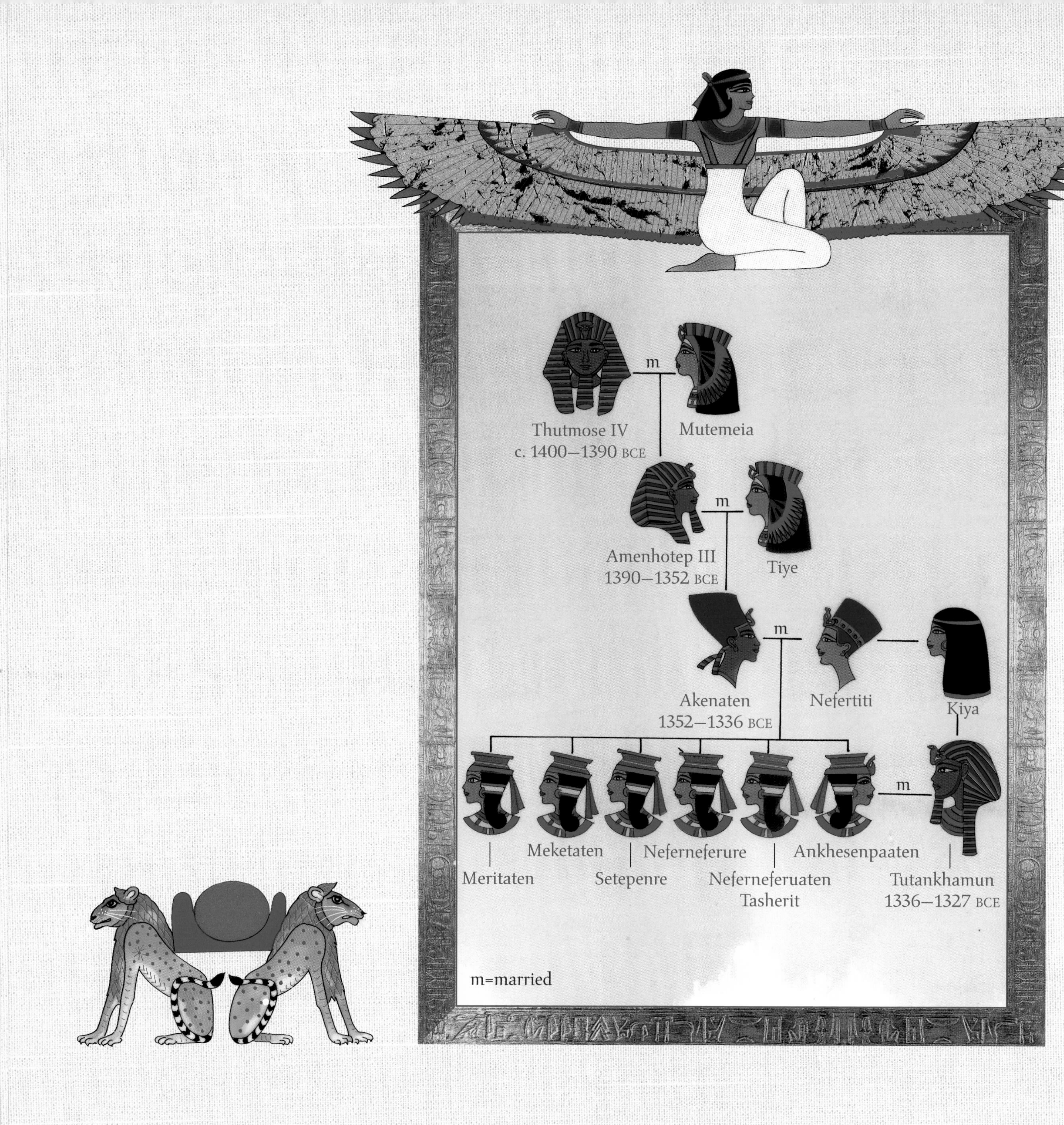
m
Thutmose IV
c. 1400–1390 BCE
Mutemeia
m
Amenhotep III
1390–1352 BCE
Tiye
m
Akenaten
1352–1336 BCE
Nefertiti
Kiya
m
Meritaten
Meketaten
Setepenre
Neferneferure
Neferneferuaten
Tasherit
Ankhesenpaaten
Tutankhamun
1336–1327 BCE
m=married

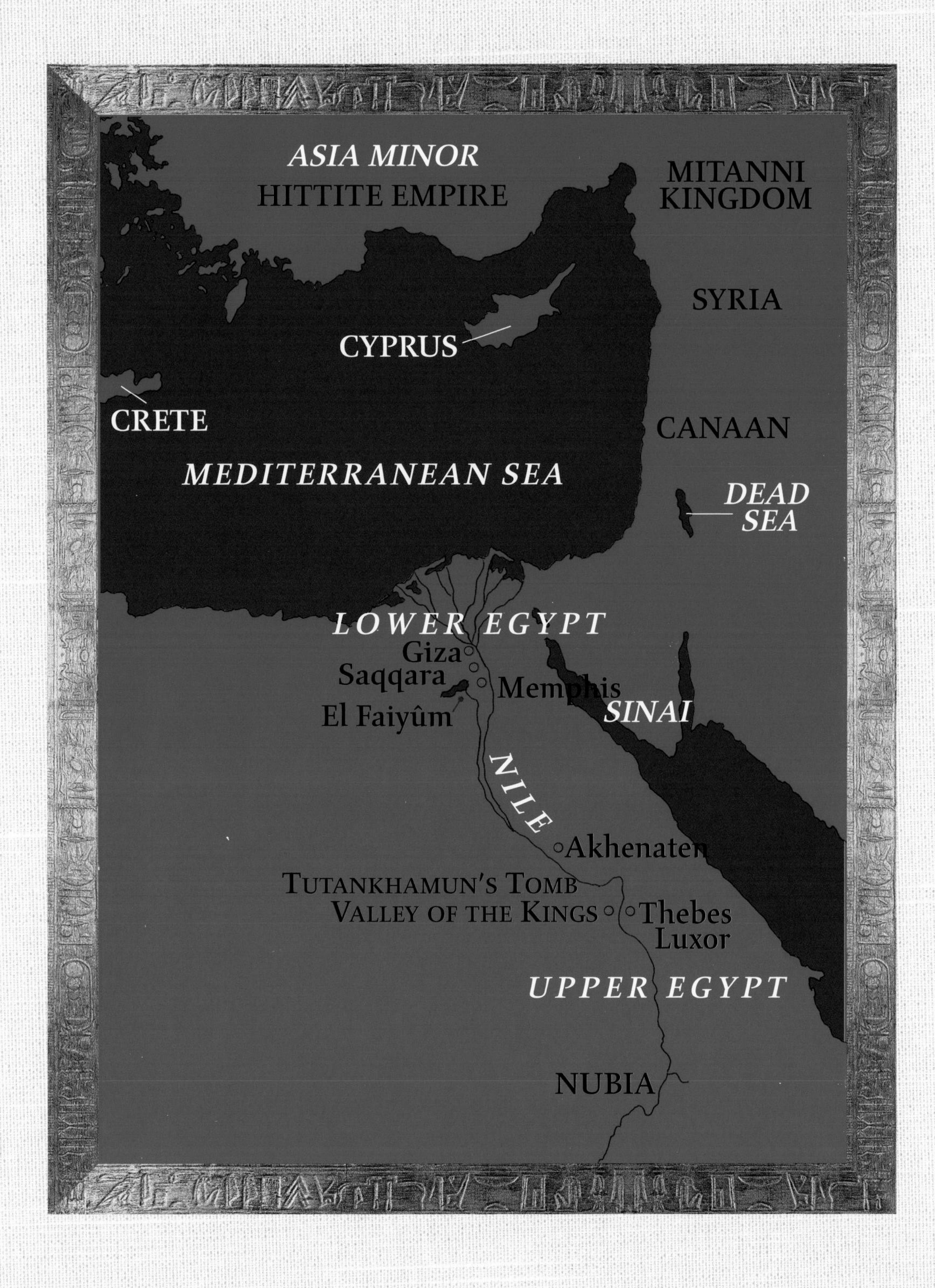
ASIA MINOR
HITTITE EMPIRE
MITANNI
KINGDOM
SYRIA
CYPRUS
CRETE
CANAAN
MEDITERRANEAN SEA
DEAD
SEA
LOWER EGYPT
Giza
Saqqara
Memphis
El Faiyûm
SINAI
NILE
Akhenaten
TUTANKHAMUN'S TOMB
VALLEY OF THE KINGS
Thebes
Luxor
UPPER EGYPT
NUBIA